SCOTLAND IN OLD PHOTOGRAPHS

INVERNESS & DISTRICT

NIGEL DALZIEL & JOHN MACKENZIE

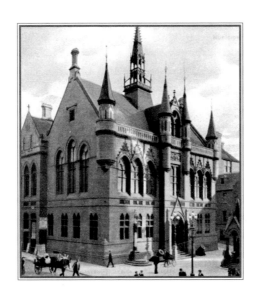

SUTTON PUBLISHING LIMITED

Sutton Publishing Limited
Phoenix Mill · Thrupp · Stroud
Gloucestershire · GL5 2BU

First published 1998

British Library Cataloguing in Publication Data
A catalogue record for this book is available from the
British Library.

ISBN 0-7509-1544-7

Typeset in 10/12 Perpetua.
Typesetting and origination by
Sutton Publishing Limited.
Printed in Great Britain by
Ebenezer Baylis, Worcester.

To the memory of a devoted Invernessian,
Alexander MacKenzie (1902–1987)

CONTENTS

Station Square and the Cameron Monument, *c.* 1918.

INTRODUCTION

To the visitor Inverness is a particularly attractive town in a stunningly beautiful location. To anyone who delves a little deeper into the origins of the place its attractions are immediately enhanced. To Samuel Johnson, in his visit in 1773, Inverness could 'properly be called the Capital of the Highlands. Hither the inhabitants of the inland parts come to be supplied with what they cannot make for themselves: hither the young nymphs of the mountains and valleys are sent for education . . .'. Here in a few brief words, he neatly summarizes the economic and social significance of the town at the start of the modern period. Although modern students may not be pleased to be termed nymphs, it is a description of the town which could almost equally apply today.

But Johnson's words belie the drama and richness of Highland history. The town lay at the heart of affairs from the earliest times as chief stronghold of the Picts and later Gaelic Mormaers, or provincial governors. From the Middle Ages it was developed as the centre of royal power in the distant and turbulent northern province. Inverness became a royal burgh in the reign of King David I (1153–65) and its importance grew as the centre of developing communications and trade throughout the region.

Despite this significance it remained a small settlement until quite recent times. With the economic growth and stability of the late eighteenth century the population rose to 10,750 in 1811 and to 20,855 in 1891. The townscape changed accordingly. The new stone and slate dwellings from the sixteenth century onwards, many of them town houses of the lairds and aristocratic families of the region, have contributed much to the attraction and character of the town. Today only a handful survive. This wholesale decimation (certainly in the 1960s, although it was also a feature of nineteenth-century Inverness) is a constant source of regret to those who have known the town over a long period. It remains a standing indictment of the planning authorities and their supporters and a convincing reason for the maintenance of strict conservation controls.

After the failure of the Jacobite revolt in 1746 and despite the subsequent repression and infamous clearances, the late eighteenth and early nineteenth centuries were a period of steady development throughout the region. Trade slowly increased and was helped by widespread agricultural improvement, although there were some places like Cromarty which declined for particular reasons.

The towns welcomed new industries, banks, medical institutions, schools (particularly in Inverness), libraries, institutes, churches and other public and private buildings. In the countryside, villages such as Kingussie and Newtonmore were developed. Social conditions were often less than satisfactory, however. Many young men from the region's growing population enlisted in the army – an obvious escape for those affected by the clearances – and Inverness itself became a port of departure for those forced to seek new lives in North America and elsewhere. Others who made made their fortunes in the empire and foreign trade, such as James Fletcher of Rosehaugh, returned to local estates in some style and their wealth generally benefited the region.

The improvements to the roads and harbours associated with Wade and others in the eighteenth century were developed further to allow a network of fast mail-coach services to be introduced to Perth, Aberdeen and Thurso by 1820. The Caledonian Canal, passing along the Great Glen and through Fort Augustus, was opened in 1822 and forged new links with Glasgow and the West of Scotland. In 1847 four steamships were operating services to Glasgow which took two days. Sail and later steam packet services from Inverness harbour operated to Leith, London and Aberdeen and fed into a network of services in the Cromarty and Moray Firths. It all reflected and encouraged economic development.

The coming of the railways was the most important single change that took place in the region, inaugurated with the line between Inverness and Nairn in 1855. In a short space of time Inverness consolidated its position as the communications hub of the Highlands and lost its remoteness and insularity. Railways certainly promoted new development and particularly the town's engineering industry. Other centres benefited: Dingwall's role as a market centre, especially for cattle, developed strongly; Invergordon was established as a major naval base and even Nairn assumed a new importance as a seaside resort for the newly mobile citizens of Inverness.

The tourist industry which began to emerge in the eighteenth century now became a major feature of the region's economy. In 1847 George Cameron published the *History and Description of Inverness*, the first guide book to concentrate solely on the town and county. Resorts such as Aviemore and Strathpeffer grew rapidly and numerous hotels were built in Inverness and in every town in the region for the benefit of both tourists and commercial travellers.

Improved access, royal enthusiasm for the Highlands and the popularity of hunting led to the great period of the sporting estates which played a major part in the social life and employment of people in the region. Traders in the towns came to depend on the estates and even local architects, including Alexander Ross and others mentioned elsewhere in these pages, were dependent on the wealthy country lairds and proprietors for a large portion of their work.

Shopkeepers also benefited from the large number of visitors to the Highland capital and surrounding towns. Many of the photographs in this book were produced for postcard purposes and they offer a fascinating insight into what appealed to our forebears and the tourist market up to a century ago. Many were taken by local photographers and publishers such as Urquhart of Dingwall and David Whyte of Inverness, but larger national firms were successfully competing for the huge market in postcards before the First World War. The cards were often over-printed with the names of retailers, mostly stationers, booksellers and newsagents.

This book hopefully provides a flavour of life in Inverness and its wider district in the early years of the twentieth century. A great deal has changed since these photographs recorded brief moments in the life of the Highlands so long ago.

CHAPTER ONE

INVERNESS

Inverness, 1954. This view nicely shows the town in its important geographical setting near the mouth of the Ness and close by the Moray Firth. Sea communications and maritime trade were an important factor in the growth of the town from ancient times. From 1675 the harbour was developed in the vicinity of Waterloo Bridge (1896) and the railway bridge (1862), the lowest crossing of the river. Stones for the construction work were taken from the nearby Citadel, the pentagonal-plan fort of 1652–5, commonly known as Cromwell's Fort. Beyond is open farmland on what is known as the Longman, an area of reclaimed tidal islets and channels. Part of this flat open area was used as Inverness's first airfield, but it is now given over to industrial uses and of course the Kessock Bridge and the A9. It was also the site of public hangings in the early years of the nineteenth century, although these were mercifully few. The last occurred on 16 October 1835 when John Adam, convicted of murdering his wife, was hanged in front of a crowd of 8,000 people.

Opposite. High Street, early 1900s. The most prominent building, centre right, is Grant's Tartan Warehouse, on the corner of Castle Street, built in 1868 and surmounted by statues representing the Three Graces. In 1911 it was claiming to be 'the acknowledged house for variety and quality combined with popular prices' for all tartans, tweeds and outdoor wear. It was demolished in 1955. The complementary classical building opposite with the prominent portico is the Bank of Scotland, built as the head office of the Caledonian Bank in 1847.

Queen Mary's House at the bottom of Bridge
Street. When Mary was refused access to
Inverness Castle in 1562 by the Constable
Alistair Gordon, she lodged here until her
army captured it. The Constable was hanged.
The building and the adjoining eighteenth-
century houses were sadly demolished in an
act of gross vandalism sanctioned by the
Secretary of State for Scotland in 1968.
Further up the street, on the site of the
medieval tolbooth, is the happily surviving
burgh steeple of 1791, although the spire was
rebuilt in 1816 following earthquake damage.
This was the year Patrick Sellar, the infamous
factor for the Sutherland estates, was tried in
the adjoining courthouse (this side of the
steeple) on charges of 'culpable homicide,
fire-raising and cruelty in the 1814
Strathnaver clearances', as a memorial plaque
on the steeple now records. Although he
succeeded in replacing the population with
sheep and in being acquitted of the charges,
'he stands guilty in the memory of the
Highland people'.

The Town House, facing the burgh's original market-place known as the Exchange, 1909. To the left is Castle Street. The Town House was the centre of burgh administration and was built between 1876 and 1882, when it was formally opened by HRH the Duke of Edinburgh. It was built in Flemish-Baronial style by local architects Matthews & Laurie and cost £13,500. In 1894 a further £500 was spent refurnishing and enlarging the Council Chamber, where on 7 September 1921 the British cabinet met to discuss Irish affairs. It was a convenient location for its members who had largely decamped to various Highland estates for the summer. Outside the building, on the left of the door, stands the old Merkat Cross, right, probably dating from the late sixteenth century. It was restored at the expense of Robert Finlay, MP for the Inverness Burghs, and located in its present position in 1900. Into the top step was set the Clachnacuddin, or stone of the tubs, originally sited in the street and where, supposedly, servants and lasses rested their tubs or pitchers of water from the river. Another theory is that it marked the site of ancient Christian baptisms. Opposite the main door of the Town House was also situated the Forbes fountain of 1882 given to the burgh by Dr George Forbes, son of an Inverness doctor who died in a cholera epidemic in 1832. George and his brother established the Inverness Dispensary for the Poor and he later prospered in the employment of the East India Company. The truncated fountain now languishes at the end of Ladies Walk beside the Ness.

High Street looking west towards Bridge Street and the 150-ft steeple opposite the Town House. On the right, at the corner of Inglis Street, is the shop of John Forbes, hosier and draper. Opposite, beside the route leading up Market Steps, is MacDonald & Mackintosh, grocers, wine and spirit dealers.

Academy Street was first laid out as a main thoroughfare in 1765. It became the town's principal shopping street and entry to Inverness for visitors arriving by train. To the right is the Station Hotel with Station Square beyond. Opposite, on the corner with Union Street, is the Royal Hotel, and on the left of the picture is the grocery shop of William J. Maclean, dealer in wine and spirits.

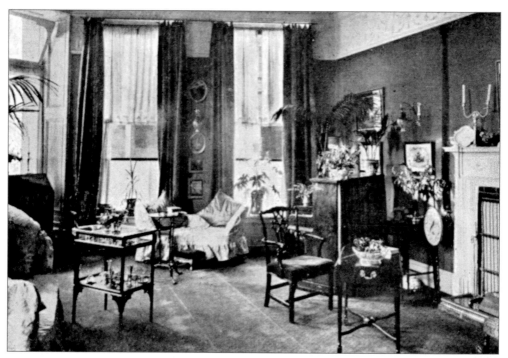

The Royal Hotel was one of many such institutions catering for the growing number of visitors and tourists to the Highlands following the opening of the railway to Inverness in 1855. The hotel was built in 1864 to the design of John Rhind and these interiors display the popular taste and decor of 1903. The drawing room, top, has a decidedly feminine and civilized feel compared with the masculine smoking room with its leather chairs and assorted weaponry. The dark interiors beloved of the period were relieved a little by a marvellous polychrome tiled floor in the entrance hall, the walls of which were also decorated with the obligatory antlers. In 1925–6 a double room cost 12s, breakfast 3s 6d and dinner 6s 6d, generally cheaper than the Station Hotel opposite.

Academy Street, which marks the eastern boundary of the medieval royal burgh – originally a wooden palisade and ditch. On the left is the massive octagonal tower (1897) of the East Church, and beyond it the site of the old Royal Academy (1792), which gave the street its name, and Station Square. On the right is the remarkable Central Hall Picture House of 1912, which was the town's only concert hall from 1931 until sadly it was demolished in 1971.

Farraline Park off Academy Street, originally Dr Bell's school, designed by William Robertson in Greek Revival style and completed in 1841. Dr Andrew Bell was born in St Andrews, became a Church of England clergyman and made a fortune while in East India Company employment. When he died in 1832 he left £120,000 in stocks for founding several educational institutions in Scotland, including Inverness. In 1937 it became a courthouse and in 1980 the public library.

A delightful photograph of Inverness station in the early years of the twentieth century. The railway opened on 5 November 1855 with a connection to Nairn. The whole of Inverness took the day off in celebration and a special train, mostly comprising simple trucks fitted with temporary seats, ran to the seaside. Thousands gathered along the route and the passengers were excited and thrilled at travelling at up to 30mph. Inverness continued to develop as the focus of railway lines extending throughout the north. The route from Nairn to Keith and connection with the Great North of Scotland's network opened in 1858; the Inverness & Perth Junction Railway in 1863; and to the north the Inverness & Ross-shire Railway opened to Dingwall in 1862 and onwards eventually to Wick and Kyle of Lochalsh. Out of this confusing number of companies emerged, through a process of amalgamation, the great Highland Railway Company with its headquarters and workshops in Inverness. Not surprisingly, the railways became a major employer in the town. The photograph looks towards the main station buildings from the westerly platforms added to accommodate the Ross-shire trains from 1862. To the left is the line to Aberdeen and Perth.

Two views of Station Square in the early years of the twentieth century. Above is the main entrance to the station (1855) designed by the Highland Railway engineer Joseph Mitchell, but sadly mutilated in the 1960s. To the left, on the north side of the square, is the head office (1873–5) of the railway itself. Hansom cabs wait beside the Cameron Monument, erected by the 79th Queen's Own Cameron Highlanders in memory of their comrades who died on campaign in Egypt and the Sudan between 1882 and 1885. It was unveiled by Lochiel, chief of Clan Cameron, on 14 July 1893. The south side of the square, below, was occupied by the railway company's Station Hotel, completed in 1859 in grand Italianate style. In Mackenzie's guide to Inverness of 1896 the manager, Edward Cesari, was advertising 'very moderate' tariffs in an hotel 'patronised by their Royal Highnesses the Prince and Princess of Wales, and other members of the Royal Family, and by most of the nobility of Europe'.

This trade photograph of 1910 advertised the offices and services of Duncan Duffy, insurance and shipping agents, 12 Lombard Street, Inverness. The high levels of emigration from the Highlands in the period are signalled in the advertisements for shipping lines serving Australia, New Zealand, the United States, South America and the Caribbean. A more middle-class clientele is being encouraged to cross to the Continent by the Dover–Ostend service in order to visit the great Belgian Exhibition of 1910. This was one of the most important expositions of the pre-war years and featured grand displays of industry and empire from all the major European states. One hopes the Highland visitors went to the exhibition before 14 August when the central gallery, much of the British section, the City of Paris Pavilion and the French restaurant were burnt down.

Crown School, known as the High School when this photograph was taken in 1913. The author's father, Alexander MacKenzie, was a pupil here at the time. It replaced the old High School in Ardconnel Street and was designed by John Rhind. Although sometimes dismissed as 'institutional Gothic', it is a fine-looking building with its dominant four-storey tower, and was erected between 1878 and 1880.

Queensgate looking west towards Church Street. Queensgate runs between Academy and Church Streets and was laid out in 1884 by Alexander Ross. From 1885 his office was located here in an Italianate Renaissance-style building in the street he himself designed. The best building, the GPO, completed in 1890, was sadly demolished in 1966 to be replaced by an exceptionally unsympathetic piece of modernism. Samuel Davidson, butcher, occupied the prominent site on the corner of Academy Street, below the offices of the General Accident Fire Assurance Corporation (resident secretary Richard Duffy).

Union Street, seen here in 1904, was laid out in 1863 on the line of an earlier alleyway leading off Church Street. All the buildings were erected in the 1860s and form a remarkable unity. Much of the north side was designed by Alexander Ross and William Joass. The Waverley, later Douglas, Hotel occupies the south side nearest Church Street, built to the design of William Laurie. The Royal Hotel, designed by John Rhind in 1864 with alterations by William Mackintosh in 1872–3, has a strongly Italianate façade and powerful roofline. The hotel's main entrance was opposite Station Square and there were frontages on both Academy and Union Streets. Interiors of this hotel can be seen on page 12. A fine row of shops shelter from the sun behind their awnings, including a newsagent and stationer and Fred J. Kelly, hatter and hosier.

Bank Street beside the Ness. These buildings were largely swept away in 1968, although the one on the corner of Bank Lane has survived. It was erected in 1804 and has been the office of the *Inverness Courier* since 1838. Carriages line the street opposite, probably cabs waiting for a fare from residents of the Caledonian Hotel to the right beyond Bank Lane. Fares were regulated by the burgh and were calculated from the Exchange. In 1911 a 5-mile trip to Culloden Moor was 6s, upriver to the Ness Islands 1s and to the top of Tomnahurich Cemetary 1s 6d.

Douglas Row, left, looking back towards Bank Street, c. 1903. The row of small-scale vernacular houses dating from the late eighteenth century is a remarkable survival today. Dominating the scene are the spires of the Free North Church (1890–3) and St Columba High Church (1851–2), originally the Free High Church, which was badly damaged by fire in 1939 but was happily restored between 1948 and 1953.

Fishing at Friar's Shott, the stretch of water opposite Huntly Street, 1904. The name is derived from the Dominican friars whose community was established near the High Church, probably in 1233. They owned property in and around the town including the fishing in this pool in the River Ness. The rights became privately owned and in the mid-nineteenth century the fishery was leased to Mr Andrew Hutcheson, an auctioneer. According to John Fraser in his reminiscences of old Inverness, Hutcheson employed John Fraser and Sandy Maclennan as fishermen and one-legged John Paterson to mend the nets. They used a seine net to catch a rich harvest of salmon and sea trout. A traditional sturdy flat-bottomed boat known as a coble, seen here, paid out the long net as it was rowed across the river. The net hung vertically in the water and as the boat rapidly cut across the current to return to shore downstream, the fish were caught in the resulting net bag. The boat was beached and the rope from the net was attached to a winch, right, known as a 'crab', which helped the fishermen to haul in the catch.

The Caledonian Hotel, seen here before the First World War, fronted Church Street and had a magnificent outlook over the Ness. In an advertisement in Mackenzie's guide to Inverness of 1896 the proprietor, George Sinclair, boasted of a 'magnificent ladies' drawing room' with the 'view from the windows being unsurpassed and extending to upwards of fifty miles of the surrounding strath and mountain scenery of the great glen of "Caledonia"'.

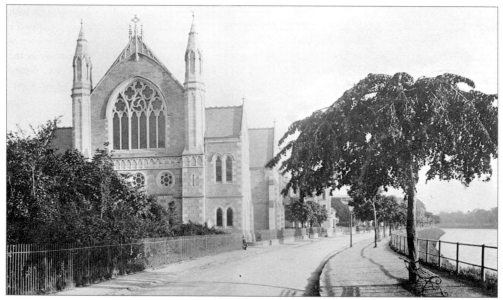

Ness Bank Church, originally United Free, designed by William Mackintosh and built in 1900–1. It lies on one of the pleasantest streets in Inverness, whose attractive houses date from before 1820 right through the classic period of Victorian design and construction.

The Flora Macdonald statue, on the south side of Inverness Castle (centre right, above) facing along the Great Glen. In the months following the collapse of the Jacobite rebellion in 1746, Flora Macdonald was one of many responsible for assisting the escape of Bonnie Prince Charlie. He was disguised as her maid and ferried across to Skye. Dr Johnson rightly predicted that she would be mentioned in history and, 'if courage and fidelity be virtues, mentioned with honour'. Her statue was only the second public monument in Inverness (after the Cameron statue in Station Square) erected by the Town Council at the direction and expense of Captain J. Henderson Macdonald of Caskuben, Aberdeenshire and the 78th Highlanders, who left a bequest of £1,000 for the purpose. It was unveiled with full civic ceremony by his daughter, Mrs Fraser, on 26 July 1899 in front of thousands of enthusiastic spectators and, according to Provost Macbean, 'in the name of Celts scattered throughout the world'.

Inverness Castle and Ness Bridge at about the time of the First World War. The castle was probably founded in the reign of David I (1124–53) and from here royal power was exercised in the region. It was eventually blown up by Jacobite forces on 20 February 1746. The site was bought by Inverness County Council and the Sheriff Court House built during 1833–6 in English Gothic style by William Burn. In 1848 the jail was added to the north side. The Ness Bridge – the main road bridge across the river – was almost as important a symbol of Inverness as the castle. The suspension bridge was built in 1855 with a magnificent battlemented arched pylon at the east end, providing a traditional and imposing entry to the town. It was demolished in 1959 and was replaced by Sir Murdoch MacDonald & Partners' existing concrete span, officially opened on 28 September 1961.

The war memorial set in the attractive and peaceful surroundings of Cavell Gardens at the end of Ness Bank. It was erected in 1922 and commemorates the dead of both world wars. The red sandstone cross was designed by John Hinton Gall.

The view west of the town showing the castle, lower left, and on the opposite side of the Ness the cathedral with the Bishop's Palace, Eden Court, beyond. Behind the cathedral is the Northern Meeting Park. Much of the area in the centre of the photograph is occupied by fine houses, designed by Alexander Ross (1834–1925) in the 1860s. The 1855 suspension bridge was replaced by a temporary structure, seen here to the left, when demolition began in 1959 in favour of the existing concrete span.

The two grand hotels on Ness Walk were built on the site of Ness House, a mansion built in the mid-eighteenth century by Colonel Baillie of Leys and demolished in 1870. The Victoria Hotel, designed by Alexander Ross, was built in 1881. The extension, with an arched pend or alleyway under, seen here, was built in 1938. The Palace of 1890, designed by Ross's firm, Ross & Macbeth, has a magnificent Scots baronial entrance reminiscent of Fyvie Castle in Aberdeenshire.

The Alexandra Hotel (previously the Victoria) before it was greatly extended on its south side. It changed its name with reigns, becoming the Alexandra under Edward VII and the Columba in 1923. At this time, before the First World War, it was the headquarters of the Scottish Automobile Club, and its proprietor had the distinctly un-Invernessian name of Mr C. Oberbeck.

When this photograph was taken at the start of the twentieth century, Ness Walk was just that, a cobbled walkway along the west bank of the river. Now the fine trees and wall on the left have gone and it is a common roadway. It was laid out at the end of the eighteenth century and was formerly part of the Muirtown estates, later acquired by Sir Alexander Matheson of Ardross. The walk has always offered some of the finest views of the castle.

The band of the Cameron Highlanders entertains the crowd before the sports commence at the Northern Meeting Park. This was the venue for the outdoor events of the Northern Meeting, a combination of Highland games and a season of balls held in September, formerly regarded as the most important social event of the Highlands. Its origins can be traced back to 1788 and it has been disrupted only twice – in 1832 because of cholera and in 1900 because of the Boer War. Beyond is the cathedral, considerably shorter than originally intended, owing to the absence of the 100-ft high spires which were intended to cap the chunky western towers.

St Andrew's Episcopal Cathedral, built in Decorated Gothic style between 1866 and 1869, is regarded as the masterpiece of Alexander Ross, the Inverness architect whose work dominates the town. It is built of pink sandstone but the nave piers, seen here, are of Peterhead granite and the altar and pulpit, to the left, are of Caen stone. The adjacent Bishop's Palace, also by Ross, is now part of Eden Court Theatre, with its chapel acting as the green room, an interesting change of use of which Victorians, and Ross, might not have approved!

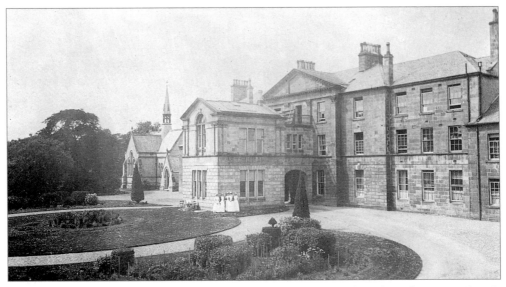

The Royal Northern Infirmary on Ness Walk was founded at the end of the eighteenth century. The side pavilions were heightened to three storeys in the 1860s and the central projecting block was added later, incorporating a *porte-cochère* with an operating theatre above. The Tweedmouth Memorial Chapel, seen beyond, was added at the same time (1896–8), the nave dedicated for Presbyterian worship and the transepts for Episcopalian and Catholic use. A commemorative plaque records that the hospital was opened in 1803.

The old Bught Mill was one of a number of meal mills in the vicinity of Inverness. It was first recorded in 1232 and known as the Mill of Kilvean, the name of the estate south-west of the town centre. The lands were bought in 1923 from Colonel Warrand by Inverness Town Council, which used the water in the widened mill lade to generate hydro-electric power. The new powerhouse built in 1929 still survives as a refreshment kiosk in the much-developed Bught recreation ground.

General's Well on the west side of the Ness opposite the islands, *c.* 1912. The well (or spring), lower left, is probably named after General Macintyre who lived at nearby Bught House in the nineteenth century. The well may have early Christian significance. A commemorative drinking ladle was provided in 1872 by Kenneth MacKenzie before emigrating to America, a fact recorded on a plaque at the well given by his son Robert, of Cleveland, Ohio. The graceful suspension footbridge designed by James Dredge was erected in 1853–4 after the two main bridges were swept away in the great spate of 1849.

The Ness Islands, seen here in about 1908, were an attractive recreation area for the citizens of Inverness. They were promoted in all the visitor guides and had a long-standing popularity. In the seventeenth century the burgh magistrates apparently gave 'open-air entertainments' here to the visiting judges of assize. On the east side of the river the Inverness Gas & Water Company had a pumping station to feed water uphill to the town reservoir on the Old Edinburgh Road.

The islands, according to the Ward Lock guide of 1925–6, are a 'unique and lovely feature which no visitor should miss . . . and are a favourite resort in the summer evenings'. The paths on the islands lead into Ladies Walk on the east side of the river and continue up to Ness Bank and Inverness itself. The walk was laid out in 1818 by Dr John Inglis Nicol, who died in 1849 during one of the town's periodic outbreaks of cholera.

Ness Castle, Inverness, lies 2½ miles south of the town and was originally known as Darrochville. This grand-looking house with its Doric portico is described as a cottage-villa and was built in about 1820 for Lady Anne Maitland, wife of Robert Fraser of Torbreck. The style was more informal and less pretentious than many classical buildings of the period; it was altered in about 1855 to an Italianate style, also evident at nearby Dochfour.

CHAPTER TWO

LOCH NESS &
THE CALEDONIAN CANAL

Clachnaharry, c. 1919. The village lies at the entrance to the Caledonian Canal and on the line of the main road and railway west of Inverness to Beauly and beyond. Its name in Gaelic means 'watch-stone', after a huge conglomerate rock which overlooks the village and where once a lookout was kept for marauding Highlanders heading towards Inverness. From the late eighteenth century Lower Clachnaharry formed a compact community engaged in fishing in the Beauly Firth and later further afield. The Muirtown Basin lies off to the right.

Shipping in the canal locks at Muirtown with the road swing bridge beyond and the Glenalbyn distillery visible, centre right, beside the Muirtown Basin. The government-financed Caledonian Canal was a triumph of civil engineering. It was designed by Thomas Telford and William Jessop and built between 1803 and 1822, connecting a series of lochs 60 miles along the geological fault of the Great Glen between Inverness and Fort William. It allowed vessels of up to 500 tons to sail in safety from one side of the country to the other, avoiding the dangerous Pentland Firth and hazardous waters around the north of Scotland.

Fishing vessels in the locks at Muirtown. The canal was of great benefit to north-east fishermen because it allowed them to better exploit the west-coast fishing grounds, particularly for herring. The Peterhead-registered sailing drifter *Ocean's Gift* (PD451), above, was owned by W.M. Forman of Buchanhaven in 1903. Steam vessels were slowly taking over from sail and in the foreground, below, is the *Coral Bank* (FR12), built by Geddes at Portgordon in 1914 and scrapped in 1948; and *Eglise* (FR102), built by Herd & Mackenzie at Findochty in 1914. These vessels were owned by J. and A. Duthie, respectively, of Inverallochy.

Muirtown Wharf at the northern terminus of the Caledonian Canal in the early years of the twentieth century. In the absence of a railway line to the south-west along the Great Glen, waterborne services prospered. Travellers arriving at Muirtown were greeted by a phalanx of cabs and carriages, above, waiting to take them on their onward journey. Carruthers' guide to Inverness of 1911 stated: 'Tourists are aware that there is in Inverness a large selection of First-class Hotels. An omnibus from each of the leading Hotels awaits the steamers, and "boots" attend the railway trains.' The Royal Hotel omnibus can be identified second from right. Below, the PS *Gondolier* (see page 42) arrives at the wharf sometime in the 1920s.

The basin at Muirtown was intended to be the second harbour for Inverness and to cope with the large trade expected on the canal. It was 800 yards long by 140 yards wide, but in the end ships outgrew it. The whitewashed cottages and workshops associated with canal maintenance activities were situated beside the second lock. Here the PS *Glengarry* is tied up, possibly undergoing maintenance herself or at the time of her disposal in 1927 (see page 41).

The Muirtown Hotel, Telford Street, *c.* 1908. It was situated close to the road bridge across the canal and was known as the Canal Bridge Hotel before 1860. The proprietor was James Sutherland, who developed the Glenalbyn distillery nearby in 1840 and became provost of Inverness. The hotel's name changed in 1900, and when this photograph was taken the proprietor was Mrs Laing.

Inverness-registered fishing vessels returning to Muirtown apparently fulfilling the Brahan Seer's prediction – 150 years before the Caledonian Canal was built – that vessels would one day sail past Tomnahurich, the hill in the photograph. Inverness fishing boats exploited the west-coast fisheries but around thirty vessels also used Loch Dochfour as well as Muirtown Basin as a sheltered winter anchorage. To the right is the canal bridge-keeper's house of 1813.

Tomnahurich cemetery. In Gaelic the name means 'hill of the yew tree', although it is commonly said to be 'hill of the fairies' – with whom it is strongly associated in local folklore. The hill is a prominent landmark and in the seventeenth century it provided a natural grandstand and course for horse races around its base. In 1863 it was acquired as a cemetery and became the main burial ground for the growing town of Inverness. The well-wooded hill remains a most attractive resting place.

Dochfour House, before 1916. It was built in Italianate style for local landowner Evan Baillie in 1839–40 by William Robertson and incorporated an older unpretentious laird's house of about 1770, left. This attractive house was further extended in the same style in 1871.

The steamer *Gondolier* at Foyers Pier, *c.* 1900. Foyers was always a popular tourist destination because of the famous waterfalls which had attracted Boswell and Johnson, Burns and many others. In 1896 the waters encouraged William Murray Johnson to build here the first hydro-electric plant in Britain, which was used to produce aluminium. Today the water, which falls 200 ft from Loch Mhor, is used to produce electricity for the national grid. Through harnessing the waters, however, the Falls of Foyers have become a shadow of their former selves.

The Loch Ness monster shot to worldwide fame in 1933 when supposed sightings, reported in the *Inverness Courier*, were taken up by the national press and by the local MP Sir Murdoch Macdonald who claimed to have seen it. The story worked wonders for local tourism and must rank as one of the most successful promotional campaigns ever.

The road from Inverness heading towards Drumnadrochit which was greatly improved in the inter-war years. Urquhart Castle is just visible at Strone Point in the distance. The headland was fortified in the Dark Ages but most of the present ruins date from the fourteenth century. In 1509 James IV gave the castle to the Grants who owned Glen Urquhart for 400 years. In 1689 government forces held out against the Jacobites, but slighted the castle when it was evacuated in 1692 so that it could not be used by enemy troops.

At the mouth of Glen Urquhart lies Drumnadrochit. The attractive sub-Baronial style hotel was built in 1881–2 and was well patronized by visitors arriving at Temple Pier 1½ miles away on Loch Ness. Fishing and walking were the main attractions, including the route up to the hill fort on Craig Monie, left, named, so legend has it, after a Viking raider defeated in battle there and killed at Corriemony further up Glen Urquhart.

The village of Milton in the fertile, sheltered Glen Urquhart, 1920s. The newly established Forestry Commission bought the southern slopes of Glen Urquhart from the Countess of Seafield in 1923. By 1975 the estate covered 26,745 acres. In the foreground are the traditional corn stacks which only disappeared with the introduction of the baler and the combine harvester in the 1950s.

The steamer *Glengarry* arriving at Invermoriston pier 6 miles from Fort Augustus. Many of the piers on Loch Ness were built by steamboat operators Hutcheson and MacBrayne during the late nineteenth century and were an important focus for local trade and tourism. As late as 1925 the Ward Lock guide to the Highlands described 'the passing glimpse of Glen Moriston from the deck of the steamer [as] one of the most memorable views of the passage through the canal'.

Gondolier entering the wide expanses of Loch Ness at Fort Augustus. The loch is 22 miles long and generally 600–700 ft deep, although it reaches 970 ft south of Lewiston. It has the largest volume of any body of inland water in Britain.

The paddle steamer *Glengarry* (1844–1927) in the locks at Fort Augustus. She was built as the *Edinburgh Castle* for service on the Clyde and transferred to the Caledonian Canal in 1846. She later became part of the Hutcheson fleet and from 1866 operated a daily return service between Banavie and Inverness in conjunction with the *Gondolier*, latterly for MacBrayne's. She was disposed of in 1927 after eighty-three years of service, by which time she had become the oldest operating steamship in the world.

The MacBrayne's paddle steamer *Gondolier* (1866–1939) passing through the locks at Fort Augustus en route from Banavie to Inverness, before 1918. The lack of a through railway line made this waterborne connection an important one for passengers and freight along the course of the Caledonian Canal. This remarkable vessel was built for the service she performed from 1866 until 1939, when she was taken over by the Admiralty and sunk as a block ship at Scapa Flow. By that time she was an historical curiosity, with engine room telegraphs by Messrs Chadburn bearing the inscription 'Makers to HRH The Prince Consort'. She was an attractive vessel, 148 ft long, whose lines were spoiled by an awkwardly shaped bow and truncated stern to facilitate her passage through the locks. The building to the right with the white gable was the premises of Robert Cameron, cabinet-maker and Highland walking stick manufacturer.

The magnificent flight of six locks connecting Loch Ness to Loch Oich, 106 ft above sea level at the summit of the canal. The village was first garrisoned by government soldiers in 1716 but from 1729 a more substantial fort for 300 men was built near the loch by General Wade. It was named Fort Augustus after William Augustus, Duke of Cumberland, youngest son of George II and victor of Culloden, under which name the village now labours. In Gaelic it is known as Kilchuimen (St Cumein's church). Following the battle in 1746 government forces returned and bivouacked in 'Camp Fields', school playing fields identified here by a Tudor-style sports pavilion, bottom left.

St Benedict's Abbey and school, Fort Augustus, built largely between 1876 and 1880 on the site of the government fort. The land was given to the English congregation of Benedictines, who wished to establish a monastery in Scotland, by Simon, 15th Lord Lovat. The first of many architects employed in the project, and mostly working in the Gothic style, was Joseph A. Hansom (inventor of the Hansom cab); he was followed by Peter Paul Pugin (son of the more famous father, designer of the Houses of Parliament), who was responsible for the striking 110-ft high tower.

The Kessock ferry was the main route between Inverness and the Black Isle and was of ancient origins. It was well used by local farming folk wanting to sell their produce in Inverness but the tariffs were always a source of contention. In 1887 there was great objection to paying 6*d* for a cow, 1*d* for a sheep and 2*d* for carrying 'small pigs in bags'. The ferry was privately run until Inverness and Ross local authorities took control in 1939. They ran it until the Kessock Bridge was completed in 1983. The pedestrian ferries above, at South Kessock in the 1920s, were replaced by vehicle ferries after the war, below. The *Eilean Dubh* took eight cars which, in 1959, cost 3*s* for the ½-mile journey. Because of her mechanical unreliability she became known as the 'ailing doo', but in 1967 she was replaced by the larger *Rosehaugh* and was made the relief boat. From 1983 she served as a tender for oil rigs in the Cromarty Firth.

CHAPTER THREE

THE
BLACK ISLE

North Kessock on the Black Isle, which developed during the early nineteenth century on land belonging to Sir William Fettes. He was responsible for building the ferry piers at both North and South Kessock in the 1820s. On the left is the Kessock Hotel opposite the West Pier, a Georgian building modified in the late nineteenth century.

The old burgh of Fortrose from the north, with Chanonry Point beyond. In the foreground is the railway station on the 15¾-mile branch line from Muir of Ord, opened on 1 February 1894, largely to exploit traffic associated with the fishing industry of Fortrose and nearby Rosemarkie. The last passenger service ran in 1951.

The ruins of Fortrose Cathedral, centre of the Diocese of Ross, which date from the thirteenth century. After the Reformation the roof lead was taken by William Lord Ruthven and decay set in. Fortunately, the North Choir range survived because the ground floor was used as a prison and the first floor as the burgh council chamber, record room and courthouse. From the seventeenth century it became the burial ground of the Mackenzies of Seaforth.

High Street, Fortrose, *c.* 1911. The village exhibited a genteel decay by the eighteenth century, but the harbour was developed from 1813 along with some linen production. Daily steamship services to Inverness later encouraged new residents and the building of large Victorian villas, all of which led to Fortrose becoming a moderately prosperous country village.

Rosehaugh, near Avoch, was one of the grandest mansions in the Highlands. Demolished in 1959, it had been designed by the architect William Flockhart for James Douglas Fletcher between 1898 and 1903. The estate was in the hands of the MacKenzies from the 1660s. Originally owned by Sir George MacKenzie, known as 'Bloody MacKenzie' for his persecution of religious dissenters, it later passed to the MacKenzies of Scatwell. The family fell on hard times and in 1864 the estate was sold to James Fletcher, who had made a fortune in the South American alpaca wool trade while settled in Liverpool. He was born in Elgin but his family regarded their roots as being in Avoch on the Black Isle, where he acquired 10,600 acres and set about creating a model estate. The house was extended by architect Alexander Ross of Inverness but was completely remodelled by Fletcher's son. No expense was spared on this lavish new building, which included sumptuous decoration, a swimming pool, Turkish bath and electric lighting. A powerhouse was built below artificial lakes and waterfalls and many estate buildings, including a remarkable dairy, were erected. The opulent lifestyle at Rosehaugh only lasted a few decades. Fletcher died in 1927, although his widow lived on at Rosehaugh until 1953. The house and estate were sold to the Eagle Star Insurance Co. and a vast sale of its contents took place. Within a few years it had been demolished.

Rosemarkie, on the route between the Chanonry Point ferry and Cromarty to the north. Rosemarkie is an ancient Christian site associated with St Moluag and St Boniface, who is said to have landed at Chanonry in the seventh century. The cathedral of Ross was established here by King David in 1125 and later moved to Fortrose.

Rosemarkie, 1910. On the left is the shop window of tailor Kenneth McRae. Dominating the village is Red Craig, a huge hill of glacial material mainly of red sandstone composition.

Cromarty Ferry, from where travellers crossed the firth to Nigg on the north shore. The route was important in the Middle Ages for pilgrims to St Duthac's shrine at Tain. The Cromarty–Invergordon ferry became the main route across the water in the early nineteenth century. In 1959 a steam launch still crossed three times daily and cost 1s 3d.

High Street, Cromarty, flanked by houses dating largely from the early nineteenth century, c. 1913. Through the two imposing gate piers, right, is Forsyth House (1770–80) built for the early promoter of Cromarty's economic development, William Forsyth.

HMS *Bellerophon* entering the Cromarty Firth before August 1913. As one of the new Dreadnought battleships, first launched in 1906, she represented the latest in naval technology. Their combination of superior speed, protection and armament (ten 12-in guns) gave the Royal Navy complete dominance at sea. *Bellerophon* was built at Portsmouth, completed in 1909 and was eventually sold in 1921 for breaking up in Germany.

Cromarty looking towards Nigg. The decayed medieval burgh was revived in the eighteenth century by local entrepreneurs William Forsyth and particularly George Ross. It became an important entrepôt for trade throughout the region and a centre for industry, including ropemaking and the spinning and weaving of flax from the Baltic. In 1785 Ross built a pier which formed the basis of the harbour, left. In the nineteenth century Cromarty's trade fell away and Invergordon became the more important port, although Cromarty continued to be used for the export of grain and livestock.

Cruisers and destroyers moored off Cromarty before the First World War. The Cromarty Firth was a favourite anchorage for ships of the Royal Navy. As early as 1854, during the Crimean War, the Baltic Fleet had over-wintered here. The ships' crews were not impressed with the town, however, which had nowhere for them to eat and the only drink to be found was whisky! From the 1860s Invergordon became the main naval port within the firth in preference to Cromarty. The latter was still used by naval vessels and sailors came ashore for rest and recreation, below. Royal Marines guarding the entrance to the firth were also stationed at Cromarty. The harbour was provided with new landing stages, lighting and crane by the Harbour Trustees, largely for the benefit of the navy, but it was little used after the war because of the collapse of the fishing industry.

A rare view of an early seaplane at Cromarty naval air station. The military use of aircraft was in its infancy when the naval wing of the Royal Flying Corps was established in 1912. Ships began to be converted as seaplane carriers, the forerunner of modern aircraft carriers. Shore bases were required for servicing and training purposes, and the first in the north of Scotland was established at Cromarty by Lt Cdr Arthur Longmore. The slipway, above, and two French-made hangars were built in readiness for three aircraft which arrived in July 1913. In August they exercised with Admiral Beatty's Battle Cruiser Squadron and in October were honoured by a visit from the First Lord of the Admiralty, Winston Churchill. He was a great supporter of the military use of aircraft and even flew in two of the planes himself. The Cromarty station was a temporary base for the aircraft, which were relocated during October and November 1913 to a more permanent and convenient home at Fort George on the Moray Firth. Subsequently, aircraft arriving in the Cromarty Firth used Delny airfield near Invergordon and later Novar (Evanton) further to the west. From 1924 the RAF used Invergordon itself as a base for flying-boat operations, for which it was particularly important during the Second World War.

Big Vennel, Cromarty, at the heart of the fishertown. Creels (baskets) can be seen in large numbers outside the homes of the fishing families. They were used for holding mussels or lug worms used to bait the hooks on hand, or sma', lines. They also held the neatly laid baited lines, which were paid out from the boats and used to catch haddock, whiting and codling. These small open boats stayed close inshore and

went out on a daily basis in autumn and winter. In 1890 around thirty boats from Cromarty were engaged in line fishing. In summer the fishermen also used drift nets to catch herring, which shoaled in huge numbers around the Scottish coast.

IN THE FISHERTOWN, CROMARTY. (1)

Fishertown, Cromarty. The womenfolk had a large part to play in the success of the fishing. In addition to baiting the lines they helped their men launch and retrieve the boats, processed the catch and as late as the 1930s sold fish from door-to-door in the local area. As the herring industry developed through the nineteenth century, fisher-lassies from Cromarty and all the coastal communities were engaged to gut and pack the fish and they followed the catches around the coast of Scotland down as far as East Anglia. In 1907 over 250,000 tons of herring were salted and packed in 2½ million barrels, largely for export to Russia, Germany and Eastern Europe. The herring fishery was increasingly the preserve of the larger full-decked boats as the herring shoals were exploited further offshore. Cromarty fishermen failed to invest and lost out to Avoch in particular, which became the leading fishing port in the area. They also suffered from the competition and over-fishing that came with the steam trawlers and drifters which appeared in increasing numbers before the First World War.

The fishmarket, Cromarty, with one of the smaller inshore boats, where daily auctions took place when the catch arrived home. Increasingly during the late nineteenth century local fishermen took the catch to the main markets for sale.

Cromarty fishertown before the First World War. The fishing industry was already in decline in the early years of the twentieth century and the war undermined it even more severely. A naval anti-submarine boom was positioned across the entrance to the Cromarty Firth and the Moray Firth fishing grounds were mined. After the war the herring market in Europe collapsed and the Depression followed. Once again, Cromarty's population fell, from 2,000 in 1914 to only 837 in 1931.

MacFarquhar's Bed, Cromarty, a natural rock arch cut by the sea, named after a local merchant of the eighteenth century reputedly involved in smuggling. In the foreground is a fishing bothy and a bag net used for catching salmon, a highly prized right traditionally belonging to local lairds. Also present is a fishing coble (small boat) used in the firth for catching salmon with sweep nets. Salted salmon had been exported as far as the Mediterranean for many centuries, but from the late eighteenth century many were packed in ice and shipped south.

Hugh Miller's cottage, Church Street, Cromarty, now owned by the National Trust for Scotland. Hugh Miller (1802–56) was a local stonemason whose natural intelligence and enquiring mind led to him becoming one of the great Scottish geologists of the nineteenth century, but he was also a fine author, journalist and Free Church preacher. The cottage was built in 1711 by his great-grandfather, John Feddes, a ship's captain, and is typical of homes of the period. Hugh Miller also lived next door in a house built by his father in the early nineteenth century.

CHAPTER FOUR

NORTH

The Invergordon ferry at the pier, right, in 1921. It was first mentioned in 1179 and continued operating to Balblair on the south side of the Cromarty Firth until 1979 when the A9 road bridge was built. The ramped ferry pier built by Thomas Telford in 1817 still exists. It was completed using money from the defunct Commissioners for the Forfeited Estates, set up to administer estates confiscated from Jacobites involved in the rebellion of 1745.

Invergordon station before the First World War. The railway was extended from Dingwall to Invergordon and opened on 25 March 1863. It was delayed by the opposition of Mr MacKenzie of Findon, who apparently feared for the safety of his tenants negotiating the proposed level crossing on the Ferry Road, so a bridge was built instead. The line was continued to Bonar Bridge in 1865.

Two views of the High Street, Invergordon, looking west, disproving the idea that the camera never lies. The photograph above was taken before October 1917 but was reissued as a postcard by Valentine's of Dundee probably in the early 1920s, below, with cars expertly superimposed. The cards were sold by J. Macpherson's stationery shop on the right (see page 63, top). In the centre is the fountain 'erected by public subscription to commemorate the visit of King Edward and Queen Alexandra, 8th September 1902'. It was made of pink granite by A. MacDonald & Co. in 1904. Invergordon was a planned village on the estate of the improving MacLeods of Cadboll. Shortly after 1813 ninety-eight feus (leasehold plots) were made available for sale lining the High Street, the main thoroughfare. The ferry pier was supplemented by a new harbour pier in 1828, and Invergordon slowly began to surpass Cromarty as the main economic and social centre in the region. In 1817 Southey's verdict on Invergordon was 'an ugly village in an important situation'.

Invergordon Town Hall, right, 1920s. The curious Renaissance palazzo-style building in poor-quality
yellow stone was designed by William Joass, 1870–1. The carved figure of Neptune, reflecting
Invergordon's dependence on maritime trade and communications, occupies the pediment. To the left is
the post office. In 1911, when William MacLeod was postmaster, deliveries were advertised at 7.55 am,
11.30 am and 6.40 pm. There were six collections during the day starting at 7 am and finishing at 7.25 pm,
presumably to coincide with the train schedule. What a service!

The Royal Hotel, Invergordon, when it was rebuilt and renamed, c. 1914. It had been known as the
Victoria Hotel and could not cope with the much larger number of visitors to the village associated with
the growing naval presence.

Beyond the King Edward fountain on High Street, Invergordon, is the United Free Church, situated on Castle Road and completed in 1861. It is now the parish church. To the right of the photograph is the shop of John A. Ross, draper, 77 High Street, and to the left Macpherson's stationers and newsagents. One of the news hoardings outside refers to the local welcome given to the US flotilla of ten minelayers which arrived early in 1918. It operated from Dalmore where the distillery was converted into a huge mine warehouse. Before the Armistice was declared the vessels helped lay 38,500 mines between the Northern Isles and Norway.

The 2nd Battalion Seaforth Highlanders on their annual route march through Invergordon in 1909 or 1911. In 1909 they were delivered by train to Thurso and marched back to Chanonry Point near Fortrose, from where small boats took them across the firth to their depot at Fort George. In 1911 they marched through Easter Ross.

'Liberty' boats in the harbour, Invergordon, *c.* 1921, returning sailors to their ships after a run ashore. To the left is the steamer *Ashdene* of Sunderland. The visit of the Home Fleet was always a welcome boost to local trade and social life. In 1907, for example, forty vessels of the Home Fleet arrived which brought to 14,500 the total number of naval personnel in the firth.

A sailor's funeral at Invergordon, before 1914. In the early years of the century many thousands of naval personnel were based at Invergordon and Cromarty or visited aboard ships of the Royal Navy. Those of the service who died were given a fitting military burial in the naval sections of the cemeteries at Rosskeen near Invergordon and at Cromarty. They also accepted the remains of the sailors who died of wounds following the Battle of Jutland.

HMS *Akbar* in the floating dock, Invergordon Harbour, before the First World War. From the middle years of the nineteenth century the Royal Navy began to make regular visits to the Cromarty Firth as a large and sheltered fleet anchorage also suitable for refuelling. From the 1880s it also gained greater recognition as a strategic port in relation to the German threat, and before the First World War it was developed as a protected port with oil refuelling and ship repair facilities. Two floating docks and their associated army of 3,000 workers were kept busy repairing vessels and fitting anti-submarine devices until the dockyard closed in 1919. One of the floating docks returned to the Royal Navy dockyard at Portsmouth, the other to her Rotterdam owners. The port continued as a naval base, and during a periodic visit by the fleet in 1931 what is known as the Invergordon Mutiny took place, during which the crews refused to put to sea. Sailors objected to pay cuts of up to 25 per cent which were first confirmed to them through newspapers bought in Invergordon. When the cuts were retracted the mutiny subsided. From 1934 the port was again engaged in the build-up to war.

Invergordon Harbour was created in 1828 and extended many times during the century. The growth in agricultural trade and the first visit of the Channel Fleet in 1863 encouraged the local laird to improve it further and a railway line was laid directly to the quaysides. It was taken over by the Admiralty during the First World War and later bought (together with the Balblair ferry) from MacLeod of Cadboll in 1918 for £16,000, plus £1,000 for its intensive use during the war. The Admiralty remained in control until the Cromarty Firth Port Authority was established in 1974.

Rest room, Scottish Churches Hut, Invergordon, one of the many facilities provided for the servicemen in the area. As early as 1915 the YMCA opened a canteen and hall for 2,500 and the churches were active in the field of spiritual salvation as well as physical comfort.

Admiralty Terrace, Invergordon. With the development of the naval port Invergordon's population of 1,100 rose to approximately 20,000 living in and around the village in 1914. Land was purchased for recreation and, as here, for house-building to overcome the severe shortage of accommodation for service personnel. The decline was equally rapid and in 1918 many houses in Admiralty Terrace were quickly emptied; some were even converted into storage buildings.

Royal Navy ships lying off Invergordon. In the foreground is the pink granite war memorial erected in about 1920. Another memorial in Invergordon commemorates the loss of the 13,000-ton armoured cruiser HMS *Natal* which blew up in the firth on 30 December 1915 with the loss of almost 400 lives. Many were guests attending a Hogmanay party on board. The ship sank within five minutes and the subsequent enquiry blamed faulty cordite.

Saltburn Road and the sea-water bathing pool, Invergordon, during one of the long hot summers between the wars. It was one of the many attractions which made Invergordon a popular holiday centre for touring by car. There were also boat excursions around the firth extending as far as Inverness and Nairn.

Saltburn village, stretching along the coast road east of Invergordon. The village was also established by MacLeod of Cadboll in the early nineteenth century, possibly to house tenants uprooted by his more efficient, improved farms inland.

Invergordon Castle was demolished in 1928 after a long history at the centre of the Invergordon, or Inverbreakie, estate. Sir William Gordon and his son Sir John Gordon set about improving their lands by enclosure and tree planting in the eighteenth century. At one stage the castle was sold for debt but Sir John secured it again, remodelled it and laid out the planned village of Invergordon. By the 1790s the castle was in the hands of the MacLeods of Cadboll. In 1919 the forty-eight-bedroom mansion was sold, first to a timber merchant and then to Sir William Martineau, a sugar magnate.

The old parish church of Rosskeen near Invergordon, designed by James Smith of Edinburgh for 1,200 worshippers and built in 1830–2. The Cromarty Firth area was subject to periodic bouts of religious fervour. In 1843, during the Disruption, a mob of 200–300, using threats of violence, tried to prevent a new minister being inducted at the church. It is now disused.

Novar House, Evanton, was built in 1720 for John Munro. His nephew, Sir Hector Munro, found fame and fortune campaigning in India, and extended and remodelled the house in the later eighteenth century. Further alterations followed in the late nineteenth century. Sir Hector built a folly, the Gates of Negapatam, on the hill of Cnoc Fyrish above the house to commemorate his Indian victories.

Alness was developed by Captain Munro of Teaninich in the early nineteenth century as a local commercial centre. A number of modest nineteenth-century houses line the High Street in this picture. Its affairs came to be dominated by the Ardross estate. It expanded greatly in the 1970s when the aluminium works were built at nearby Invergordon.

The vast baronial pile of Ardross Castle was built in 1880–1 to the design of Alexander Ross for Alexander Matheson, nephew of the founder of the celebrated China trading company Jardine Matheson. His considerable fortune, gained largely from the trade in opium, enabled him to retire at the age of forty to the Ardross estate purchased from the Duke of Sutherland in 1846. He turned the lands into a model estate, mixing large with smaller holdings to help repopulate the area. It was sold in 1898 to C.W. Dyson Perrins, of Worcester Sauce fame.

When Alexander Matheson turned Tollie Lodge into Ardross Castle in 1880–1 he also had the gardens reclaimed from bog. Grandiloquent terraces were laid out with fountains, sculptures and statues. Two giant stags reflected the majesty of the Highlands as well as the stalking interests of the area.

Tarbat House was designed by James McLeran in 1787 in a plain classical style. It incorporated part of New Tarbat House which had been built by Sir George Mackenzie, Viscount Tarbat and first Earl of Cromartie, in the late seventeenth century, itself replacing an earlier castle. It has been described as 'one of the most important Georgian country houses in the Highlands'. It fell into disrepair after it was sold by the Earl of Cromartie in 1966. In 1987 it was gutted by fire and subsequent attempts to save it have led nowhere.

CHAPTER FIVE

WEST

This 1906 view of Strathpeffer Spa, with its fine Victorian buildings, reveals its character as a Highland health resort. Set in mountainous scenery, it lies in the valley below Ben Wyvis 5 miles west of Dingwall. The springs at Strathpeffer were known for their supposed curative properties in the late eighteenth century, an analysis of their composition being published as early as 1772. Their fame spread, but it was not until the 1840s that a new community began to grow up around them. By late Victorian times it had grown into one of the grandest resorts in Scotland.

An elegant Edwardian clientele gathers in the square near the Spa Building, Strathpeffer. The first pump room was built over the springs in 1819 by Mrs Hay-Mackenzie. A new pump room was opened in 1829, replaced by a grander structure in time for the boom years of the 1870s. A new stone pump room and baths were opened in 1881 but the baths were demolished after the Second World War, by which time the spa had fallen completely out of fashion.

The commercial premises in the square at Strathpeffer were built in the 1840s and are still known as the Spa Buildings. In 1911 the postmaster was William Wilkie. Hugh Beaton, as well as being the stationer and tobacconist, was also the registrar of births, marriages and deaths. Thomas Wellwood Maxwell was the pharmaceutical chemist. The Strathpeffer Free Church, built in whinstone and sandstone in 1886, was designed by the architect William Joass.

A few years later the trees had grown up and the buildings had sprouted a glass canopy; the post office had become Lady Seaforth's Institute; and A. Humphries & Co., grocers, occupied the large double-fronted shop. The Ben Wyvis garage was advertising tours in open charabancs to Kilmorack and Glen Affric.

This picture of the Spa Cottage, left, and the main bath house, right, precedes the building of the Highland Hotel, begun in 1909. The bath house was demolished in 1950, an action greatly regretted. The earlier pump house of 1839, which currently contains an exhibition on Victorian Strathpeffer, can still be seen across the road. Spa Cottage has sliding wooden shutters or jalousies, and these and other architectural features, together with mountainous scenery, 'balsamic air' and scented trees, help to give Strathpeffer the atmosphere of an Indian hill station.

Holly Lodge Hotel is typical of the smaller buildings at Strathpeffer. It was built in 1901 with fine classical features, including its Italianate tower. Its ironwork and architectural detail repay close inspection. It remains a small, comfortable privately run hotel.

The great mass of the Highland Hotel, with its Germanic towers, has now risen behind the cottage and bath house. It was built by the Highland Railway to designs by Cameron & Burnett in 1909–11. It lends a touch of Bavaria to the exotic feel of Strathpeffer.

The pavilion at Strathpeffer was opened in 1881 during a building boom in the spa village. It was used for various entertainments and dances, while the surrounding 'tastefully laid-out' ornamental gardens were ideal for those who preferred gentle strolls rather than golfing or hill walking. A guide of the 1920s announced that the orchestra played in the gardens thrice daily or in the pavilion if wet.

The Spa Hotel, the first major hotel in Strathpeffer, was opened in 1879. This apparently gave it the right to proclaim in its advertisements that it was 'the oldest establishment and leading hotel, replete with modern conveniences'. Its managing director before the First World War was Mr A. Wallace, who claimed that his hotel was situated close to the 'finest inland golf course in the North'.

The Ben Wyvis Hotel opened hard on the heels of the Spa Hotel in 1880. It has been described as resembling a 'vastly overgrown villa' and may have been designed by William Joass, who certainly added an extension in 1884. This was timely, for the branch railway line from Dingwall arrived in 1885. Soon Strathpeffer boasted a direct train service from London. The Ben Wyvis advertised itself as having 'the finest situation amidst pure bracing air' in 'scenery unsurpassed in the Highlands', with its own extensive pleasure gardens and 'a private path to the wells and baths'.

This view of Strathpeffer from the golf course on the slopes of Creag Ulladail clearly shows its spectacular setting. The Ben Wyvis Hotel can be seen with its flag flying. The tower of the Free Church is to the left, the bath house and pavilion centre right. The tower of St Anne's Episcopal Church is visible on the extreme right. It was designed by John Robertson as a memorial to Anne, Duchess of Sutherland and Countess of Cromartie, and was built in the 1890s. The Highland Hotel is absent from the scene so the photograph pre-dates 1909.

The Eaglestone, a Pictish carving at Strathpeffer, remains a favourite attraction for tourists. Judged to be about 1,300 years old, the stone displays symbols of an arch and an eagle. The eagle may have been the insignia of an important person in Pictish society. In the sixteenth century the celebrated Brahan Seer foretold that if the Eaglestone fell three times, the Strathpeffer area would be flooded. Perhaps he was anticipating global warming and the rise of ocean levels!

Castle Leod was built in the early seventeenth century by Roderick Mackenzie, younger brother of Kenneth Mackenzie of Kintail. It may have been finished in 1616 but was later extended. It was little used in the eighteenth century and was ruinous by the early nineteenth. It was restored with various additions between the 1850s and 1912, including work by the architects David Bryce and Donald Matheson. Today it is the residence of John Mackenzie, Earl of Cromartie, known as Cabarfeidh, chief of the Clan Mackenzie.

The Falls of Rogie were (and remain) a favourite destination for walks from Strathpeffer. The route lay by Loch Kinellan. The falls are on the Blackwater, a tributary of the River Conon.

The Raven Rock, or Craig-an-Fithich, is a celebrated precipice on the railway line between Dingwall and Kyle of Lochalsh, several miles beyond the station at Achterneed. When the Kyle line was first proposed the intention was to take it through Strathpeffer, but Sir William Mackenzie of Coul House objected and the line had to be routed further north over the Raven Rock summit. The station at Achterneed was known as Strathpeffer for several years until the 2½-mile branch from Fodderty Junction to Strathpeffer was opened in 1885.

The Dingwall–Foulis train snowed up on Friday, 28 December 1906. This photograph was taken by the intrepid Urquhart of Dingwall, where only two days previously the snow lay 8 ft deep. The *Inverness Courier* described the snowfall as one of the most severe of recent years. Highland Railway engines on the Skye line were given snow ploughs to negotiate the drifts but for a time it was a losing battle. The deep cutting at Raven Rock was impassable to trains where one lay entirely covered by snow up to 14 ft deep. The falls were heavy all across the Highlands but the effects were felt throughout the country. On the east coast telephone and telegraph lines were blown down, Aberdeen was cut off and in the far south even London had several inches.

Major General Sir Hector MacDonald (1853–1903), known as 'Fighting Mac', was one of the great heroes of the Gordon Highlanders, having risen from the rank of private. He was born at Rootfield near Muir of Ord, the son of a crofter-mason. Having worked in a draper's shop in Dingwall, he joined the army in 1870. He saw action in all the most important imperial campaigns of the late nineteenth century, including the Afghan War (1879–80), the first Boer War (1881), the Nile expedition (1885) and the Sudan campaigns of 1888–91 and 1896–8. He was promoted 2nd Lieutenant by Lord Roberts in Kabul in 1880. MacDonald was credited with such a skilful handling of the wing at the Battle of Omdurman (1898) in the Sudan that he turned a near disaster into a victory. He became Commander-in-Chief in Ceylon in 1902, but was accused of a sexual misdemeanour and shot himself in Paris.

Dingwall, Hill Street.

The MacDonald Monument can be seen on the hill beyond Hill Street which runs south from Dingwall town centre. The town's name derives from the Norse 'thing vollr', the meeting place or court. James Mackenzie & Sons, cabinet-makers, were to be found in the Royal Hotel Building.

The national memorial to General Sir Hector MacDonald was begun in 1904 on the cemetery hill south of Dingwall overlooking Strathconon and his birthplace at Rootfield. It was designed by James Sandford Kay and was opened on 23 May 1907.

The view of Dingwall from the cemetery hill, laid out by C.R. Manners in 1890 and capped by the MacDonald Memorial. Dingwall received its royal charter from King Alexander II in 1226, but was given a new charter in 1498 after alienation to the Earls of Ross in the fourteenth and fifteenth centuries. It stood on the River Peffery, but various attempts to turn it into a successful port failed.

Dingwall languished in the eighteenth century but began to expand in the early nineteenth. Its significance as a market town and administrative centre for Ross & Cromarty increased after the arrival of the railway in 1862, and several hotels and other public buildings were constructed in the town.

The town house, now the museum of Dingwall, is a curious mixture of styles. The central stone tower housing the original tolbooth jail was built in 1733. The steeple was added in 1773–4 and was later replaced by a wooden belfry cupola containing a hand-wound clock. The Edwardian baronial additions on each side of the tower were added by William Joass in 1902–6.

The Dingwall fancy dress cycle parade, 4 July 1917. The event was probably associated with Red Cross Week, which took place across Scotland between 2 and 8 July, during which money was raised for its important wartime work. At least one contestant is dressed as a nurse (perhaps she is a nurse), but the presence of a sign proclaiming 'Keltic Boots Tread the World' is a mystery.

The Seaforth Highlanders' Memorial Cross was originally erected at Cambrai towards the end of 1917, following the battle in which the Seaforths suffered heavy losses. A number of tribute tablets were placed on a tall cross erected on a mound of stones by both Seaforth comrades and the citizens of Cambrai. In 1924 it was dismantled and brought to Dingwall by a party of Seaforths led by Colonel T.W. Cuthbert. It was reconstructed in Station Square and dedicated in a moving ceremony attended by many of the burgh's inhabitants on 12 March 1925. At the same time the war records of the 4th Battalion, in a sumptuously bound volume, were placed in an impressive cabinet which is still to be found in Dingwall Museum. The cross has been replaced several times, most recently in 1990, because of storm damage and rot. In a town which boasts several war memorials, this one, with its informal origins in France, is particularly evocative.

The National Hotel in Dingwall, with its broad overhanging eaves, dates from 1858. The First World War memorial by J.J. Joass, 1922, consists of a bronze statue of a kilted soldier.

The original leaning monument in Dingwall was erected to commemorate George, first Earl of Cromartie, Viscount Tarbat, Lord MacLeod and Castlehaven, who died at Tarbat House in 1714 in his eighty-fourth year. He was buried close to the monument. His lead-lined coffin was found in 1875 and the memorial plaque was renewed by Roderick, Earl of Cromartie, in 1876. The monument was rebuilt by Sibell, Countess of Cromartie, in 1923. The original monument stood 65 ft high and leaned 5 ft to the north. The rebuilt version is half the original size.

Muir of Ord was virtually the creation of the railway. The village developed after the opening of the Inverness–Dingwall line in 1863 and grew further when it became the junction for the line to Fortrose on the Black Isle in 1894. Mackenzie's butchers seems to be one of the most prominent shops on the High Street.

Brahan Castle, about 4 miles south-west of Dingwall, was a tower house built for the Mackenzies of Kintail and Seaforth in 1621. It was greatly enlarged and extended in the late eighteenth and early nineteenth centuries but is now demolished. On the estate worked Coinneach Odhar – Kenneth Mackenzie, the Brahan Seer – who accurately foretold the fall of this powerful family. Much about his existence remains a mystery but he is generally said to have been born at Baile-na-Cille, Uig, on Lewis, in the early seventeenth century, and was given a stone with which he could predict the future. His prophecies were legendary and after he became a labourer on the Brahan estate, in the vicinity of Loch Ussie, he was summoned to the castle by Countess Isabella who wished to know why her husband Kenneth Mackenzie, 3rd Earl of Seaforth, lingered in Paris. When told that he was enamoured of a French lady, Isabella's rage was such that the seer was ordered to be burned in a barrel of tar at Chanonry Point. This prompted Coinneach's prophecy that the Seaforth line would end when the last Earl, deaf and dumb, died following his four sons, which was the fate of the 6th Earl, Francis Humberston Mackenzie, who died in 1815. The seer also predicted that one of the chief's daughters would kill the other, which occurred when the Hon. Caroline Mackenzie died following an accident in a pony carriage driven by her sister Mrs Mary Stewart-Mackenzie.

Fairburn House, about 5 miles north-west of Muir of Ord, was constructed in 1877–8 for John Stirling. It was designed by Wardrop & Reid in Scottish Baronial style with neo-gothic interiors. The predecessor castle, Fairburn Tower, still stands and was built after 1542 for Murdoch Mackenzie of Fairburn.

Affric Lodge, at the east end of Loch Affric, was one of many hunting lodges built in the Highlands during the heyday of the sporting estates in the nineteenth century. The Affric and adjoining Fasnakyle estates were bought by the Forestry Commission in 1951 and form the core of an area of outstanding conservation value based on its native pinewoods.

The Glenaffric Hotel at Cannich in Strathglass. It was built in 1862 and designed by Inverness architects Matthews & Lawrie who were also responsible for Drumnadrochit Hotel. It was a favourite hotel for fishermen and those who delighted in unspoiled landscape. The remoteness of the area preserved a large swathe of important native forest from exploitation, and the pinewoods in Glen Affric were only penetrated by road in 1959.

The Fasnakyle hydro-electric power station, Glen Affric, built in 1952. According to Muirhead's guidebook of 1959 the new road up the glen to the Beneveian dam and along the loch afforded views of 'delightful scenery, a combination of sylvan beauty and mountain grandeur'. Local landownership is now dominated by the Forestry Commission which, by the early 1970s, controlled almost 70,000 acres in the Glen Affric forestry estate, allowing excellent public access.

The village of Beauly was laid out by the 14th Lord Lovat in the 1840s with a grand central square and streets leading off each side. The Beaufort estate office of the Lovats was located in the village and serviced this and several other local estates. The village was dominated by the MacLeans. In 1911 various MacLeans were grocers, blacksmith, boot and shoe maker, cycle dealer, draper and slater. Two sisters, Elizabeth and Charlotte Tulloch, ran a bakery in the square. The monument commemorates the raising of the Lovat Scouts for service in the Boer War by the 16th Lord Lovat and was unveiled in 1905.

The Lovat Arms was the main hotel in Beauly, owned for many years after the First World War by James MacLean, who catered to a 'high-class clientele'. The adjacent garage was known as Aird Motors, and W. Jepson, stationer and newsagent, was situated near the post office. In the 1890s Lord Lovat tried to develop Beauly as a spa after Dr Ogilvie Grant had analysed the waters and extolled their therapeutic value. There were stories of miraculous cures, but Beauly never rivalled Strathpeffer and its potential as a spa was soon forgotten.

Beauly Priory. The Gaelic name for Beauly was said to have been Manachain or 'place of monks', but the story goes that the monks of the priory called it *Bellus Locus*, Latin for beautiful place. Mary Queen of Scots, source of so many legends, supposedly rendered this into French as Beaulieu when she visited the priory in the summer of 1564, much taken by the beauty of its location and its fine orchard. The name is more likely to derive from the Gaelic bealaidh or 'broom'; local boys apparently used to wear the plant as a crest. The priory was founded by the unusual order of Vallis Caulium in about 1230. The ruins of the church, all that survives above ground, date from the late thirteenth century. Within are the tombs of Prior Mackenzie (1479) and Sir Kenneth Mackenzie of Kintail (1491). After the Reformation the income of the priory was given to the Bishop of Fortrose, and masonry may well have been removed to help build Cromwell's citadel in Inverness in 1653. In 1900 the north chapel was restored as a burial place for the Mackenzies.

The Phipps Institute, the rather grand public hall of Beauly, which opened in 1902. It cost £4,000, and was paid for by the tenant of Lord Lovat at Beaufort, Mr H. Phipps of Pittsburgh, Pennsylvania, who apparently fell in love with the village and its community. In addition to the hall, which could accommodate 600 people and up to 80 performers on the platform, the building contained a library, reading and recreation rooms. Phipps also gave £900 for a hall in the nearby village of Kiltarlity.

From about the middle of the nineteenth century deer-stalking became the characteristic élite sport of the Highlands. Many estates were turned over to it and hunting lodges were built throughout the region. In 1901 there were forty-two 'shootings' in the Beauly district alone and it was estimated that 4,500 stags were shot in Scotland each year. The carcases were brought off the hills by sturdy Highland ponies.

CHAPTER SIX

EAST

The battlefield of Culloden where the forces of Prince Charles Edward Stuart were defeated by government troops under the command of Prince William Augustus, Duke of Cumberland, on Wednesday 16 April 1746. It marked the end of Stuart attempts to regain the throne lost when James VII and II was deposed in favour of William and Mary in 1688. It also marked the start of a long period of repression in the Highlands as the government attempted to eradicate all opposition. The Jacobite army, predominantly composed of Highlanders, had successfully taken Charles as far as Derby before retreating north. Their epic journey, however, ended on the flat desolate expanse of Drummossie Muir which was particularly ill-suited to their style of combat and main tactic – the charge. Conversely it was ideal for Cumberland's forces, particularly the artillery, which wreaked havoc on the Jacobite force. Although tired, hungry, ill-equipped and heavily outnumbered, the Jacobites mounted an heroic charge on the government lines but were soon overcome. The 20-ft high memorial cairn, seen here, was erected by Duncan Forbes in 1881. It incorporated an inscribed stone placed there by Edward Power in 1858, which was the only memorial on the battlefield at that time. It is the location of the annual service of commemoration organized by the Gaelic Society of Inverness.

The Well of the Dead is situated in front of where Wolfe's and Barrel's government troops were positioned, on the right of the Jacobite charge. Here was found the body of Alexander MacGillivray of Dunmaglass who led the men of Clan Chattan in the main assault which broke through Munro's and Barrel's regiments in the front line of Cumberland's forces. The Jacobite army probably numbered under 5,000, of whom at least a fifth were killed in battle and in the indiscriminate slaughter that continued afterwards with the approval of 'Butcher Cumberland'. Below, a military commander from another age, Lord Roberts of Kandahar (1832–1914), Commander-in-Chief of the British Army and hero of the Boer War, pays a visit to the Well of the Dead and the other battlefield monuments in August 1903. What his thoughts were is not known.

Old Leanach Cottage was a farmhouse on the left of Cumberland's forces, today located beside the visitor centre operated by the National Trust for Scotland which owns the site. Its associated outbuildings have gone, including a barn where it is said thirty Jacobite officers and men were burned alive by government troops after the battle. The cottage was inhabited until 1912.

The Cumberland Stone, a huge conglomerate boulder which was once said to be the position from which the Duke of Cumberland directed the battle. This is now thought unlikely, although he may have surveyed the field from this position or even hurriedly eaten here after the battle.

King's Stables, Culloden, which marks the position of Cumberland's dragoons who were given the task of guarding the battlefield after the conflict ended. A number of memorial stones were placed on the battlefield in 1881 by the Laird of Culloden, Duncan Forbes, principally marking the graves of the clans but also including the English Stone (near to the Well of the Dead), which marked the grave of many of the 364 government soldiers who died out of a force which numbered up to 9,000.

The old Culloden House, where Bonnie Prince Charlie stayed before the battle, was demolished in 1772 and replaced by the present building, seen here, in 1780. It was the seat of Duncan Forbes, 5th Laird of Culloden, on whose land the battle was fought. As Lord President of the Court of Session and Scotland's premier judge he was a strong government supporter, but even his appeals for clemency for defeated Jacobites were refused by Cumberland. The original basement rooms survive where Forbes' steward concealed eighteen Jacobite soldiers after the battle. The rebels were eventually discovered and executed.

Culloden railway viaduct across the River Nairn on the section of the Highland Railway line between Daviot and Inverness, finally completed in November 1898. The sandstone viaduct of 29 arches, 700 yards long, was a major feat of engineering design by John Fowler and Murdoch Paterson. The line required the excavation of 2 million cubic yards of rock and spoil, the building of four major viaducts and cost £1 million.

Ardersier was originally a planned village established by the Campbells of nearby Cawdor and named Campbelltown. It apparently merged with the nearby village of Stuarton established by the Stuart Earls of Moray. It sat astride the ancient highway striking northwards by way of the headland, where Fort George lies in the distance, and the ferry across the Moray Firth to Chanonry Point on the Black Isle. The last regular ferryman died in 1932, when the service ended.

Fort George on the Moray Firth opposite Chanonry Point. The fort was built after the 1745–6 Jacobite rebellion as part of a major scheme to pacify the Highlands, and it has been in military use ever since. It is now regarded as one of the most impressive fortifications of eighteenth-century Europe. To the left of the fort are the remnants of a seaplane base, first located here in 1913.

Fort George was completed in 1769 and took twenty-one years to build. It was designed by William Skinner, appointed military engineer for north Britain and made first Governor of Fort George for his services. The governor's house is on the left of this main west range next to the artillery block (1762–6). All the fort's brick and mason work was undertaken by John Adam, brother of the famous Robert and James.

The 2nd Battalion Seaforth Highlanders parading at Fort George, between 1909 and 1912. The battalion returned to its home area and regimental depot at the fort following a spell of duty at Edinburgh Castle, where they were occupied with training as well as parading with the 3rd (Special Reserve) Battalion. The Seaforths were established in 1881 as an amalgamation of two regiments of foot founded by the Mackenzie Earls of Seaforth in 1778 and 1793, when the government was desperate to utilize Highland manpower during the American and French wars. The troops are drawn up on the parade ground inside the main gate of the fort, right. Beyond is the north curtain wall, joining the Duke of Cumberland's bastion off to the right, where troops were housed in casemates – vaulted rooms under the ramparts protected from gunfire. Each casemate held up to forty men. Altogether the fort housed 1,600 men plus the resident artillery unit on a site of 42½ acres. It was a huge construction project for its day and the eventual cost of building the fort was more than double the original estimate of £92,673 19s 1½d.

Staff block, Fort George, *c.* 1904. The main range of buildings north of the artillery block, overlooking the parade ground, housed the fort's administrative staff and storekeepers with houses, right, for the Lieutenant-Governor and the Fort Major.

Maxim machine-gun team at work on the butts near Fort George. The Maxim gun was a devastating weapon which helped give British troops a powerful advantage on many imperial campaigns. At the Battle of Omdurman, for example, the 1st Battalion Seaforth Highlanders faced the main Dervish attack which never got closer than 800 yards, because of the murderous rate of combined rifle and machine-gun fire.

Kilravock Castle on the west bank of the River Nairn near Cawdor, owned by the Rose family since the thirteenth century. The fine towerhouse was built after a licence was granted by the Earl of Ross in 1461. It was further extended in the seventeenth century. In 1746 Prince Charles Edward Stuart stayed here two days before Culloden, and the Duke of Cumberland the day after.

The royal burgh of Nairn obtained its foundation charter in the Middle Ages and it became a significant market town in a fertile agricultural area. Between 1818 and 1825 Thomas Telford straightened the River Nairn and built a quay on the new channel. A further quay was added on the opposite bank in 1830 from where the locally caught herring and white fish were exported. Some shipbuilding took place there and Nairn was visited by steamers on the Inverness, Aberdeen and Leith service.

By the late nineteenth century Nairn, seen here probably in 1928, had become a favoured holiday resort. Its low rainfall and mild climate, together with its golf courses, swimming pool and beach, attracted visitors from throughout the region and beyond. For the citizens of Inverness it was a short rail journey away, ideal for a day trip.

Nairn's almost empty High Street, 1905. The Waverley Hotel was built in Italianate style in 1877 and marked the growth of the town in the later decades of the nineteenth century. The Highland Hotel beyond was built in 1896. Donald Grant MacKenzie, a wine and spirit merchant of some note, occupied no. 42 within the Waverley building. His next-door neighbour, J. Munro & Co., fruiterers, had ceased to trade by 1911. Beyond can be seen Harrison's Library & Newsagency, which later moved to the station, and Alex Nicol, grocer.

An early open touring motor sweeps down Nairn's High Street in this view dating from 1906, but the girl still feels bold enough to pose for the photographer in the middle of the street, watched by some male bystanders. The fine architecture and elegant layout of Nairn are well represented in this photograph.

In the days before oppressive levels of traffic, Nairn High Street had a quiet and dignified air. Important public buildings, such as the Court House of 1817–18 and the public hall of 1865, were located here as were most of the principal shops. In the early years of the twentieth century Lipton's grocers stood at no. 80 in a fine palazzo, as ever publicising special teas. Beyond, at no. 82, was Greenlees & Sons, boot manufacturers.

Nairn was proud of its parish church. It was built between 1893 and 1897 to the design of John Starforth of Edinburgh and followed late Victorian preference for a powerful Gothic Transitional style, with double transepts and a confident parapeted tower. It cost £9,500, was constructed on a site presented by Lt-Col. Clarke of Achareidh and could accommodate 1,200 worshippers. It replaced an earlier parish church of 1809–11 which remains ruinous.

The Golfview Hotel seen here in the inter-war years. It was built with additions between 1890 and 1897 to the design of Duncan Cameron and stands between the firth and the golf course that gave it its name. By 1911 the town had three courses, one of eighteen holes and two of nine holes, one of which was the ladies' course.

Darnaway Castle near Forres, home of the Earls of Moray. The present house was designed by Alexander Laing and built between 1802 and 1812, but incorporating Earl Randolph's Hall of the 1450s with its great carved oak roof. James IV gifted Darnaway to his mistress, Lady Janet Kennedy. Mary Queen of Scots dispensed justice here in 1564.

CHAPTER SEVEN

SOUTH

Leys Castle, 2½ miles south of Inverness, a neo-gothic pile with a delightful conservatory attached. The heavily turreted and crenellated mansion was built in about 1833 when the style – exemplified by the Houses of Parliament (1839–52) – had become highly popular. The 'castle' was built for Colonel John Baillie by Samuel Beazley, who it comes as no surprise to learn was a London playwright and theatre architect.

Moy has been the home of Clan Mackintosh chiefs since the fourteenth century. Bonnie Prince Charlie was entertained here in February 1746 by Lady Anne Mackintosh, a staunch Jacobite, whose husband (the clan chief) was fighting on the government side. The prince narrowly avoided capture by Lord Loudon's government soldiers, who were sent hurriedly from Inverness to intercept him. 'Colonel Anne's' five picquets used cover of darkness to convince the troops they were facing the entire Jacobite army, and the result is known as the Rout of Moy.

Carrbridge, like Aviemore, developed with the building of the direct railway line between Inverness and Perth in 1898. In 1896 Mackenzie's *Guide to Inverness* stated: 'the first section of six miles (from Aviemore) already open to Carrbridge, where also there is a very good and well-kept Hotel' – the Carr Bridge Hotel, left – which was extended in 1892 and 1911. To the right is the main road bridge south over the Dulnain, a tributary of the Spey.

The Carr Bridge Hotel, 1929. To the right is the new bridge built in 1928 to replace a previous structure (see above). To the left is an even older bridge of 1717 from which the village took its name. It was built by John Nicolson of Pluscarden for £100 which was paid by the Earl of Seafield, the major local landowner. Although the specification insisted on a structure of sufficient height and span 'as will receive the water when in the greatest speat', its parapets were washed away in the great flood of 1829.

The remains of the Batan railway bridge across the Baddengorm Burn in the aftermath of what the *Inverness Courier* described as 'one of the most distressing accidents in the history of the Highland Railway'. During the afternoon of 18 June 1914 a cloudburst created a flash flood of considerable force which washed away the road bridge between Tomatin and Carrbridge. The debris was carried downstream and lodged between the piers of the railway bridge, 1 mile west of Carrbridge, creating a temporary dam approximately 20 ft deep. The water undermined the bridge piers and the subsidence derailed the 11.50 am train from Perth to Inverness, which was brought to a halt halfway across the bridge. Shortly afterwards the bridge collapsed and three carriages were thrown into the water. One carriage broke in two and half of it was deposited a

quarter of a mile downstream. Many passengers had lucky escapes but five drowned: W.J. Morrison (auctioneer), Duncan Macpherson (steamer agent), both of Inverness, Miss May Guthrie of Colinton (niece of Lord Guthrie) and Mr and Mrs Waithman of Hurstview, Chudleigh in Devon. Survivors were taken to Carrbridge, Aviemore and Inverness suffering from shock and minor injuries except for Mrs Maclennan, wife of the stationmaster at Auchterneed, who was severely injured and taken to the Royal Northern Infirmary in Inverness. News of the tragedy caused widespread concern, reflected in the *Courier's* publication of two later editions of the newspaper in addition to the normal print-run of 4,500 copies.

The great North Road at Slochd, 1930s, with the railway viaduct on the line from Carrbridge to Daviot opened in 1897. The railway reached its highest point nearby, on Slochd Mhuic summit, 1,315 ft above sea level. The eight-arch viaduct was over 100 ft high and involved two deep cuttings. In Gaelic Slochd means pit or hollow, and the gorge was originally a channel formed by glacial meltwater.

The Cairngorm mountains under snow and Nethy Bridge, seen from above Broomhill station on the opposite side of Strathspey. The area gave its name to the 'strathspey' dance, which is in slower time than the reel, invented locally in the eighteenth century. The long line and curve of the parallel Spey Valley railway can be seen in the centre of the view. Broomhill station was on the line from Boat of Garten to Forres, which closed on 18 October 1965.

The Nethy Bridge Hotel, begun in 1898, was described in the guide books as a 'first-class hotel' with a nine-hole golf course, fishing rights and, of course, tennis. It was also ideally located for access to the walks in the Abernethy Forest and the Cairngorm range, and was 'one of the spots from which the ascent of this mountain can be conveniently made' (1925–6).

The Cairngorms have attracted many visitors over the years but not all have been allowed to enjoy them at their best. This is the grave of Hugh Alexander Barrie near Aviemore, which also commemorates Thomas Baird interred at Baldernock, who both lost their lives on 2 January 1928 while climbing these hills.

Easter Aviemore, *c.* 1910. Aviemore today is a sizeable mountain resort, but it was a late creation of the railway when the main north line was pushed through from Perth to Forres in 1863. It developed further when the more direct branch was built from Aviemore to Inverness via Carrbridge (1892–8).

Before the arrival of the railways, according to the Ward Lock guide to the Highlands (1925–6), Aviemore 'consisted mainly of a general shop, a post office, and an old inn, in which Burns had stayed. There are now many handsome villas and several hotels', including the Cairngorm Hotel which dates from about 1900 and which has an attractive tower and elaborate barge boarding. The Station Hotel is beyond.

Station Hotel, probably just after the First World War. The railways encouraged travel to the Highlands and really opened up the region for the first time. It was trumpeted in the guide books as an excellent base for attempting the summits of the Cairngorms as well as for more sedate recreations, including bowling. Golf courses soon developed and in the 1920s the Rothiemurcus Club was happy to charge visitors 1s a day or 8s 6d for a fortnight. Visitors to the Station Hotel had exclusive use of a small course under Craigellachie crag to the rear, the latter described as a trysting place of Clan Grant whose war cry was 'stand fast Craigellachie'. Their territory extended to the other Craigellachie 30 miles north-east at the foot of Strathspey. The village prospered further in the 1920s and 1930s with the advent of motor car touring.

Loch Polladdern above Aviemore and the Spey valley from Craigellachie. The Station Hotel is prominent and the station itself lies only 100 yards down to the right. Today the busy A9 sweeps across the foreground, the land on this side (to the west) now being designated a National Nature Reserve.

This monument was erected to commemorate James Martineau LLD, DD, DCL, STD, LiHD (1805–1900), Unitarian minister and educator who became Principal of Manchester College. He was the brother of the celebrated Harriet Martineau, writer, social reformer and friend of Wordsworth. He retired to the area, living for many years at the Polchar. The monument was restored in 1974 by the Scottish Unitarian Association. A memorial also records the contribution of his daughters to the life of the community: Mary Ellen founded a library for the use of the people of Rothiemurcus and Gertrude and Edith taught wood carving.

Duke of Gordon Hotel, Kingussie, *c.* 1918. The village lies at the head of Strathspey and although of ancient origin it was laid out and developed by the 4th Duke of Gordon, who offered plots of land for sale from 1799. He hoped to develop a local textile industry but was unsuccessful. The opening of the railway between Inverness and Perth in 1863, and its later extension, led to Kingussie developing a new role as a holiday centre. The hotel was designed by Alexander Cattanach and opened in 1906.

The Duke of Gordon Hotel lounge. Guide books invariably complimented the wonderful environment of Kingussie. Its clear air and aroma of the surrounding pinewoods were considered 'highly beneficial to sufferers from chest complaints' (1925–6). As late as 1959, however, Muirhead's guide recorded that 'visitors are discouraged from straying on the mountains, which are preserved as grouse-moors and deer-forests'. Instead, visitors to the hotel could look at the stags' heads and use their imagination.

The neat and refined drawing room of the Duke of Gordon Hotel. It was a large and spacious hotel and the interiors were an obvious source of pride to the proprietors and managers, Mr and Mrs Wolfenden, when this photograph was taken at about the time of the First World War.

The gaunt ruins of Ruthven Barracks near Kingussie, built in 1718 and now in the care of Historic Scotland. This is the best preserved of four infantry barracks built in the aftermath of the 1715 Jacobite rising and was designed to house 120 soldiers. It was captured and burned out during the later rebellion in 1746. It overlays a series of earlier castles on this site overlooking the Spey, begun in the thirteenth century.

Badenoch Highland Games underway at Kingussie in 1911. The modern gatherings originated in the late eighteenth century desire to preserve Highland culture and the martial spirit which was so highly regarded. Societies sprang up to promote these aims, including the Highland Society of London which promoted a piping competition at the Falkirk Tryst in 1781. The sporting side of the games soon took a full part in such gatherings and when Queen Victoria attended the Braemar Gathering in 1848 they were given the royal seal of approval, and remain popular today.

Members of the 4th Battalion Seaforth Highlanders and Lovat Scouts, part of the Territorial Force of reservists, attending Church Parade during the summer camp at Kingussie in July 1914. They had just returned home to the Black Isle when they were mobilized on 4 August 1914 at the start of the war.

King Street, Kingussie, in the early years of the nineteenth century. To the right is C.C. Irvine's boot repair shop. As it is a planned village the streets are neatly laid out. Its most famous resident was James 'Ossian' Macpherson (1736–96), Kingussie schoolmaster and publisher of Gaelic verse in the 1760s. His new wealth allowed him to build Balavil House on the site of ancient Raitts Castle nearby.

This general view of the village of Newtonmore well illustrates its position on the edge of the mountains and passes of Badenoch. Major William Caulfeild's military road from Crubenmore to Kingussie passed through Newtonmore in the early 1760s and gave the village its strategic significance. A crofter's blackhouse lies in the foreground.

Newtonmore was created by James Macpherson, the son of the eighteenth-century scholar, administrator and writer of 'Ossian' fame who settled at the nearby estate of Balavil. Gardens and woodland among the scattered villas provide an attractive rural feel to this part of the village in a photograph dating from the 1920s.

Newtonmore lies at the foot of the fine steep slopes of Craig Dhu, seen here in the distance. An hotel stands at each end of the main street, the Balavil Arms here at the east end built in 1900 and the Craigmhor to the west. Most of the buildings in the village's main street are typical Highland vernacular of the nineeenth century. Craig Dhu Lodge, near Newtonmore, was the home of Captain Fitzroy RN, the master of HMS *Beagle* at the time of Charles Darwin's famous voyage to the South Pacific.

The characterful face of a Highland shepherd in traditional tartan plaid, *c.* 1902. Sheep were widely introduced to the Highlands during the clearances which continued from the late eighteenth century up to the 1850s. As a cure for the problem of overpopulation, periodic famine and unprofitable estates, landlords began the widespread eviction of tenants which verged on genocide. The significant revolt in 1792, the Year of the Sheep, was easily suppressed and not repeated. The land was given over to black-face and Cheviot sheep and the human populations either resettled (often on the coast and marginal land), driven to find work and shelter in the towns and cities, or forced – sometimes literally – into emigration. There was even an influx of the displaced Gaelic population into Inverness. One of the first sheep farms in the region was at Corrimony, south-west of Inverness, where trees were felled from 1797 to clear the land for grazing, but the whole of the north was badly affected, particularly Ross and Sutherland.

Although sheep remain an important part of the Highland economy, and even led to the development of woollen manufacturing in Inverness and elsewhere in the region during the early nineteenth century, they became less profitable in the middle years of the nineteenth century. Many of the estates were developed for sport instead but evictions continued. Sporting estates, however, provided opportunites for provision merchants, taxidermists and sporting stores, which sprang up in large numbers in Inverness and elsewhere in the Highlands.

A shepherd and his flock beside a blackhouse which, as an image, represents the popular view of the traditional Highland agricultural economy and domestic arrangements. However, not only were sheep an eighteenth-century introduction, but the common single-storey, whitewashed, stone house with gable chimney also appeared at the same time. Previous habitations were generally less substantial and largely built of mud, timber or turf.

ACKNOWLEDGEMENTS

The photographs in this volume have been amassed over a number of years and from a variety of sources. Our thanks are due to a number of individuals and institutions who have helped in the creation of this book, but principally to the following for advice, information or permission to reproduce images:

David Alston of Cromarty Courthouse Museum, A.D. Cameron, David Hughes and David Bertie of Aberdeenshire Heritage, Inverness Library, Kate Macpherson of Dingwall Museum, Kate Newland of the Scottish Fisheries Museum at Anstruther, the *Scottish Daily Mail* (photograph page 42) and *Scottish Sunday Express* (photograph page 24, bottom).

BRITAIN IN OLD PHOTOGRAPHS

SUTTON'S PHOTOGRAPHIC HISTORY OF TRANSPORT

To order any of these titles please telephone our distributor, Littlehampton Book Services on 01903 828800
For a catalogue of these and our other titles please ring Emma Leitch on 01453 731114